Pause and Rewind
in LIVERPOOL

Peter Burgham

Dedicated to my wife

and our family and friends

with love

PAUSE AND REWIND
in LIVERPOOL

Welcome to this short and not-too-serious poetic tour of the many-faceted and celebrated city of **Liverpool.** There are already many guidebooks about the city, but this one is perhaps a little unusual in being primarily a set of **photo-poems**. I've tried to include a mixture of aspects of the city and its environs, with a variety of styles, so hopefully there's something for everyone.

The cover image shows *The Allerton Oak*, a thousand-year-old resident of Calderstones Park. Well, it makes a change from using the *Royal Liver Building* to symbolise the city !

In **Pause and Rewind** we can perhaps take a few moments to reflect on life and especially on those values and customs which we believe make the world a better place, such as compassion, patience, tolerance and not least something Liverpool is particularly famous for, a sense of humour.

This series of books is essentially focused on *Places*. But places are not the same without *People*. Think about any football stadium during the lockdown of 2020-21 and you'll know what I mean. Liverpool has been the birthplace of many celebrated people in many spheres of activity. But it is the unsung heroes of Liverpool that this book also celebrates, 'ordinary' people with extraordinary character, who find a way to navigate life's many hurdles. It is they who inhabit these places and fill them with music and laughter and charm

There is much to be grateful for in the part of the world in which we live. The nature of progress is that it won't suit everyone, but it is inevitable and we have the opportunity to shape it. The baton will then pass to the next generation for them to apply their own ideas, and we believe in them with confidence and great hope.

*

This collection is a fusion of my own words and photographs. All the pictures are associated with Liverpool, where I was born and raised, apart from one - see if you can spot it ! Many of the poems have been newly commissioned for this book. Some of the rest have appeared elsewhere as text in my other works, plus a few from the inaugural **Pause and Rewind** (which had a wider remit).

In making the choices for the book, I've tried to reflect different interests and different moods, so that you can dip in at any page you choose, any time.

Whilst English is widely spoken on Merseyside, the indigenous language is Scouse, so I have included some translations where necessary !

Photo-poems

The idea of **photo-poems** is not new. There are examples from the 19th century, originally evolving from a type of poetry known as 'ekphrastic' in which poems were inspired by works of art. But a modern collection of photo-poems in celebration of the historic city of Liverpool possibly is a first !

The main aim of photo-poetry is to try to combine words with images in an eye-catching way. Ultimately we aspire to create something where the whole seems greater than the sum of the parts. It is true that 'beauty is in the eye of the beholder' and each of you reading/ viewing these pages will form your own opinion, see things in different ways, and that's just fine. But I hope the result in each case will be something positive and satisfying.

The good news - certainly for me - is that you don't have to be a genius to create a photo-poem. The small example above perhaps illustrates how simple it can be - a snapshot taken on a mobile phone, a little editing with the effects on the computer, and the addition of a few words to try to capture the mood, or react to the picture.

The Image and the Poem, the Places and the People, the Land and the Sea, the one helps to define the other, to see the other in a different light.

So please enjoy these photo-poems and be encouraged to create your own too - be they simple or grandiose, heartfelt or sad, profound or just plain daft !

Peter Burgham

December 2021

Poem	*Topic/Place*	*Page*
In the Centre of the Dream, a Magnolia	Royal Liver Building	7
A Million Suns *(extract)*	Sefton Park	8
Tickets Please	Lime Street Station	9
Pub Philosophy	City Centre Pubs	10
The Allerton Oak	Calderstones Park	11
Peach and Rose *(extract)*	West Kirby and New Brighton	12
Without You	Football (aka Religion)	13
Hope Street	Cathedrals	14
Circle of Life	Albert Dock	15
Dem Pomes	River Mersey/City of Culture	16
Ode to the Lamb Bananas	Super Lambananas	17
Somewhere Between an Orange and the Moon	Mersey Poets	18
The Actor In Us All	Theatres	19
Merseybeat	Beatles and Mathew Street	20
Mersey Royals	Mersey Ferries	21
Gifted Amateurs	Liverpool Cricket Club	22
Grand National Lockdown Centenary Stakes 2121	Grand National	23
Lest They Forget	War Memorial, Huyton-with-Roby	24
Mersey Air	Otterspool Promenade	25
Community *(extract)*	Liverpool Montage	26

In the Centre of the Dream, a Magnolia

Anchored high above
the celebrated waterfront
the mythical birds
stand back-to-back

    protecting the people
    and their good fortune
    an Edwardian gift
    an eternal pledge

    while down below, wrapped in fog
    that's wrapped in smoke that's
    wrapped in grime and grit
    the pool looks sound

        radiates and teems with life
        where bathed in light
        at centre stage a single tree
        invigorates the dream

Royal Liver Building, Liverpool

Note: the magnolia in the dream is a reference to Carl Jung's 'vision of Liverpool' ... the 'pool of life'.

A MILLION SUNS

They've bulbed a million suns
in the grass of Sefton Park
assembled, primed, and classified
a weapon of mass construction
an army of the heart.

Hear then this call to alms
let it trigger just one spark
one flicker of hope or foolish pride
this solar-powered beacon
this natural work of art.

In 1990, the Marie Curie charity in conjunction with Liverpool City Council planted a million daffodils in Sefton Park, and named it 'The Field of Hope'. The idea spread, and throughout the UK there are now many 'Fields of Hope'.

They've seen it all, the ticket inspectors ...

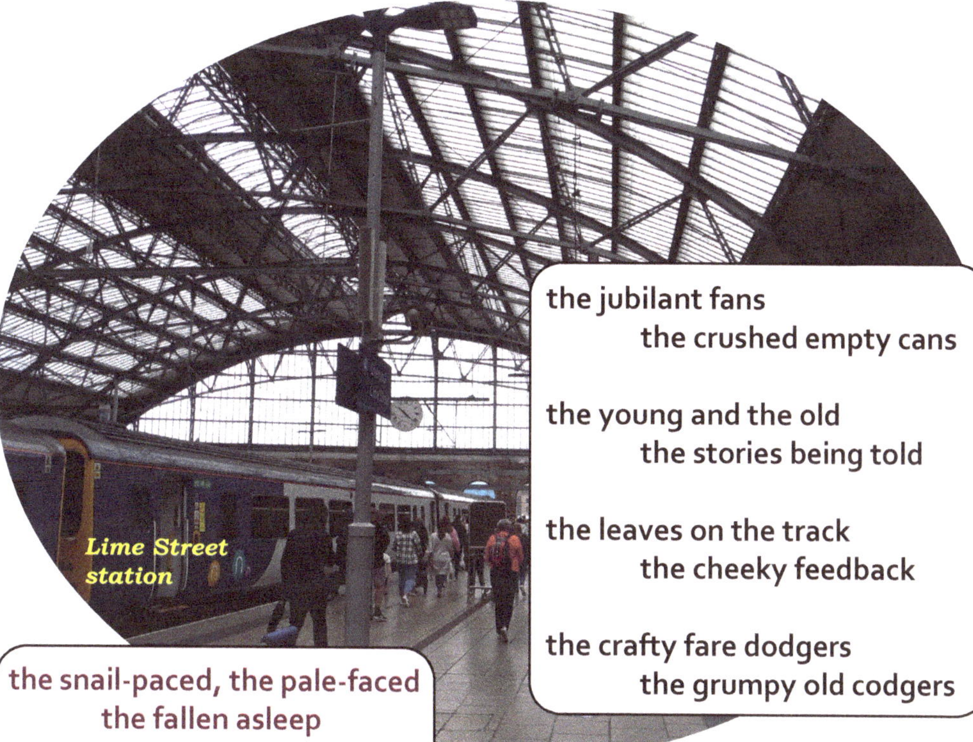

the jubilant fans
　　　the crushed empty cans

the young and the old
　　　the stories being told

the leaves on the track
　　　the cheeky feedback

the crafty fare dodgers
　　　the grumpy old codgers

the snail-paced, the pale-faced
　　　the fallen asleep

the scurriers, the worriers
　　　the text message beep

the cards on the table
　　　the volume up loud
the fake designer label
　　　the party-time crowd

the sneezes and coughs
　　　the litter on the floor
the pigs in their troughs
　　　the scrawl on the door

the wrong day of travel
　　　the payments declined
the yarns they unravel
　　　the years left behind

The Liverpool Pub is traditionally a place of great wisdom, especially after several pints of the local brew...

Truth and Lies will never cease
but only Truth can give us Peace

You may have all the facts but not all the knowledge
it's never too late to make life your college

Philosophers they're not just a part of history
they're a part of you and a part of me

There is no right there is no wrong
life is just a made-up song

so sing out loud
and sing out strong

and if your singing is offkey
we won't offend your dignity

but when your mates give you the hint
then sit down, pal, you've done your stint

Note to poets in pubs: Please rhyme responsibly...

A child lifts a fallen acorn,
looks in awe at the noble tree
holding sway like a sceptred earl,
& tightly grasps the woodland pearl.

The mighty oak's borne witness
from badger's snout & squirrel's paw
to the hundred trials of swains & lords,
the king's decrees and clash of swords.

A legend for all seasons, survivor
of storms and wars and the shipman's axe,
of mildew, moths and ordnance blast,
with epic tales of the millennium past.

And now before the court the child
swears solemn oath upon the seed,
while propped by guardians all around
the gnarled old oak defends its ground.

Peach and Rose

rainy day on the Wirral

Beside the seaside

got asked quite straight,
hey lar 'oo d'ya fink's
da prettiest, me or me mate ?

Throwaway camera to hand
I take a pretty mean snapshot,
show the photo, then all polite
slip myself out of the picture:

Ah ladies, you see my plight,
for who on earth knows
how to choose between **a peach** *and* **a rose** *?*

[extract from 'Peach and Rose' in the collection 'Bird's Eye View']

FOOTBALL

(see also 'Religion' and 'Marriage')

Football fans are noted for their devotion to their team, bordering on religious fervour. It's a brave man (or woman) who arranges their wedding day to coincide with a local derby...

a bell
without
a ring

a bird
without
a wing

a hive
without
a bee

a lock
without
a key

> Without You,
> I'd Be

a tram
without
a track

a front
without
a back

a diary
without
a date

a soul
without
a mate

a low
without
a high

a cloud
without
a sky

a spoke
without
a hub

a fan
without
a club

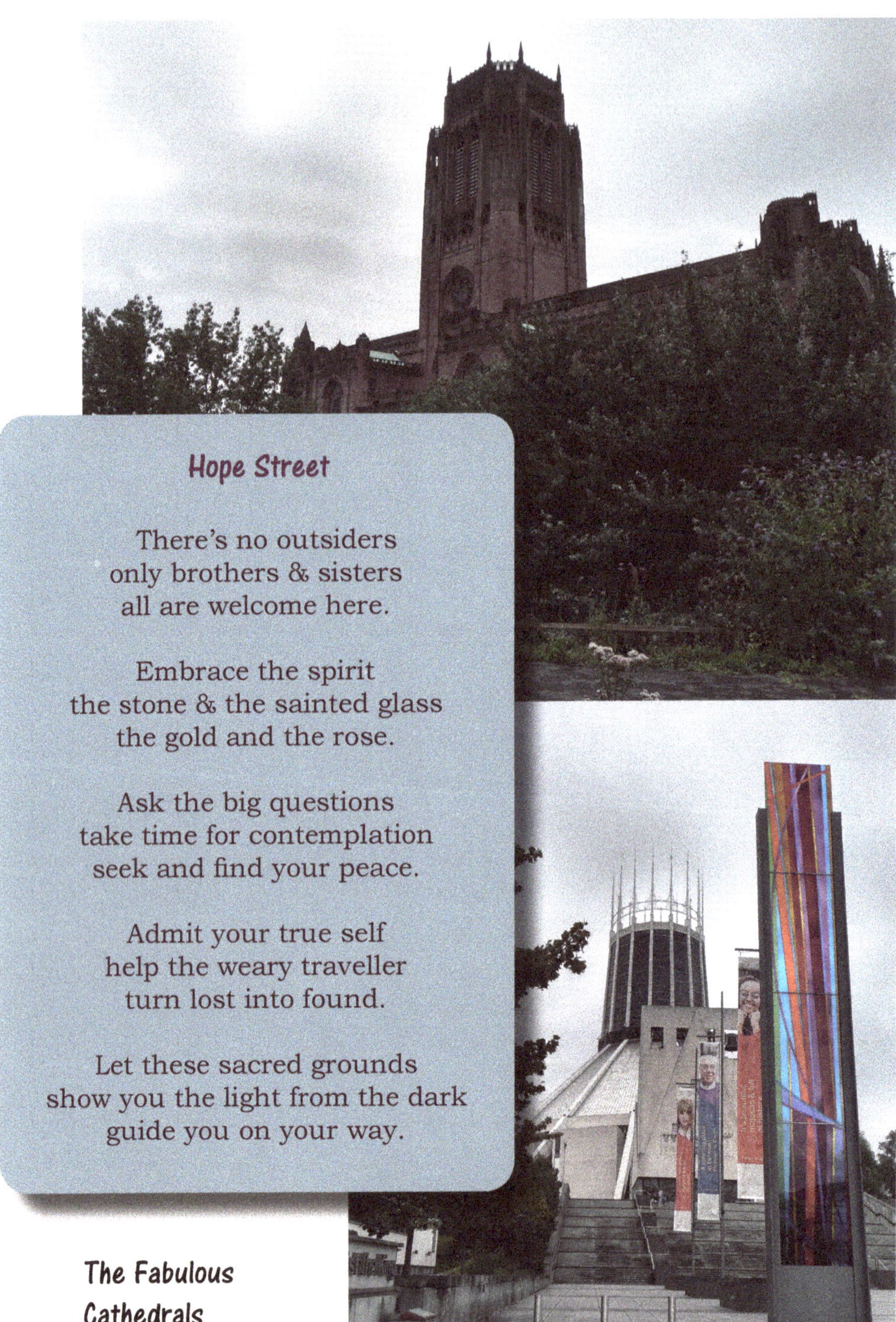

Hope Street

There's no outsiders
only brothers & sisters
all are welcome here.

Embrace the spirit
the stone & the sainted glass
the gold and the rose.

Ask the big questions
take time for contemplation
seek and find your peace.

Admit your true self
help the weary traveller
turn lost into found.

Let these sacred grounds
show you the light from the dark
guide you on your way.

The Fabulous
Cathedrals

- none to spare

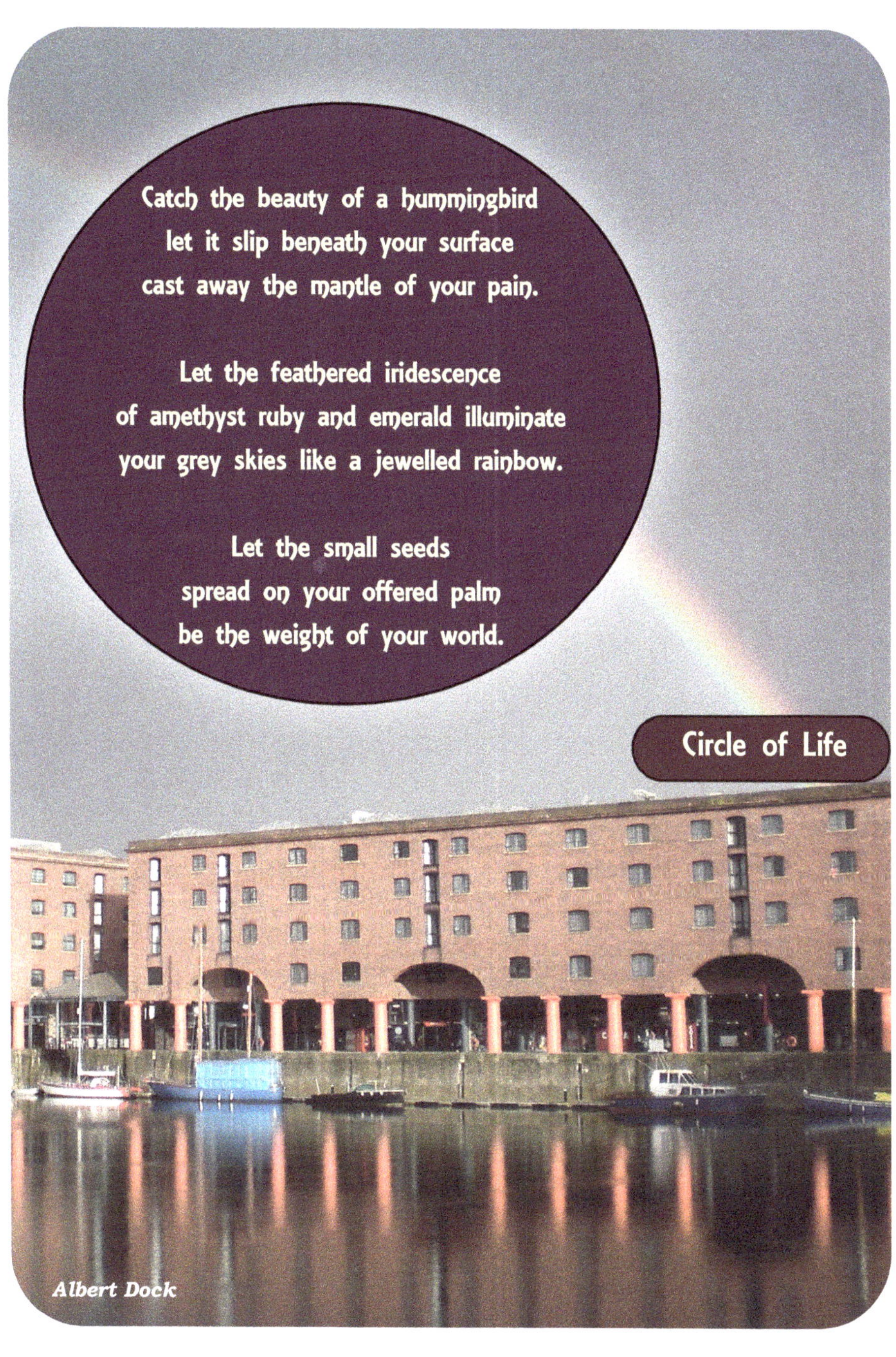

Catch the beauty of a hummingbird
let it slip beneath your surface
cast away the mantle of your pain.

Let the feathered iridescence
of amethyst ruby and emerald illuminate
your grey skies like a jewelled rainbow.

Let the small seeds
spread on your offered palm
be the weight of your world.

Circle of Life

Albert Dock

C
I
T
Y

O
F

T
H
E

P
E
O
P
L
E

Dem Pomes

Dem pomes dem pomes is in me 'ead
And softly through my dreams de tread

De ravel out dem mental knots
Give t's the cross and i's the dots

And like dem sparklers de crackle in me mind
Pyrotechnux of the cerebral kind

De take me to a magic place
Take inner fears to outer space

And like da stars yer carn explain
Nor wrap dem up in cellophane

I know yer think dat rhymes are sad
And youse may say 'been on da waccy lad?'

But let me tell yer this my friend
Da first sign of madness is when dem pomes end.

it's so cool dat da schoolkids can reach yers
and paint all them different features ...

Super Lambananas racing around the outside
of the Museum of Liverpool

[note: Becher's Brook is a famous fence on the Aintree racecourse]

Liverpool dialect:
'dead' = very

Forever remembered for its explosion of music, art and poetry.
The Beatles, Gerry and the Pacemakers and so many other bands set the scene alight.
The poem below is a concoction in homage to the Mersey Poets, influential to this day.

Somewhere Between an Orange and the Moon

I lifted an orange
and put it in my pocket
and everywhere I went
I offered it to passers-by.

But no-one would take my orange
they said it wasn't good enough
they needed something better
like pear or grass or moon.

I began to feel a sadness
for the orange
because indeed its only crime
was the abject lack of a decent rhyme …

[with due acknowledgement to Brian Patten, Roger McGough, Adrian Henri]

Those tears to me are imitation pearl,
Glass baubles manufactured on demand,
Costume jewellery for the drama queen.
A fashion show. A comedy. A performance,
Royal command.

And by your hands those promises
Discarded like cheap toys,
Theatrical props for the actress.
A puppet show. A parody. Another of your ploys.

No tears of pearl run down my cheek,
But deep inside, a drama's played,
A cast of ghosts upon an empty stage.
A mystery. A tragedy. An endless masquerade.

[extract from 'Broken Promise' in the collection 'Bird's Eye View']

A stardrop landed in a pool
of ordinary raindrops
and with its magic
made them want to dance
and sing and scream with joy.
It flowed on from the pool
in a stream of happy songs
sweeping all the other raindrops along
as it headed for the river
and the river became a torrent
that burst into the sea
that flooded into the ocean
and went right round the world
as all the droplets in all the oceans
were touched by the magic
and sang and danced
and joined as one.
Imagine ...

Merseybeat

Mathew Street area, city centre
plus Beatles statue, Pier Head (superimposed)

Mersey Royals

[... extract from Bird's Eye View...]

A duet in E flat for horn and seagulls,
mournful notes across the silt, an evensong
for the last in line of the Mersey monarchy.

Fragile circumstance and faded pomp
unfurled with undiminished pride. The ancient
right of passage of man and horse

ordained by royal charter, a ferry tale,
a commoners' tale of humble service
recounted from Domesday to Zeebrugge.

Steam power taming tide and time
until the tunnel vision of rail and road
brought its unrelenting storm.

Sunset over the river, gone now
the *Egremont* and the *Leasowe*,
the legacy reduced to dim-lit memories,

the famous *Royal Iris* rocked into legend,
long since abandoned and rusting alone,
the chords a distant echo.

Gifted Amateurs

In praise of amateur sport on Merseyside, a great tradition and source of comradeship, sportsmanship, banter and plain old common sense ...

(i.m. Ralph Owen)

The king of the wing Arnold Dingle
was as Scouse as the old Pier Head
the 'Scouse Pearl' indeed on a good day
but more often he just stayed in bed.

A footballer down to his bootstraps
he'd shout "over 'ere son on me 'ead"
but you don't do headers in hockey
as poor Arnie wished someone had said.

The Mersey Archers
maybe missed their aim
when first they thought upon a name
perhaps they met up in a pub
the day they formed their angling club

A prominent batsman in cricket
the ball he would whack it and flick it
but one day he was out
to a very odd shout
when his wig fell down onto the wicket

A powerful lad from Edge Hill
once headed the ball with some skill,
it went into space
at a fabulous pace
that new star in the sky is our pill

Club colours ! The author played hockey for many years for Liverpool Sefton H.C. based at Liverpool Cricket Club.

Liverpool dialect: 'pill' = a football

Grand National at Aintree

Grand National
Lockdown Centenary Stakes 2121

A cyber horse number 5952
will win the National
ridden by cyber jockey 1984
on a cyber course in a cyber place
watched by a global cyber audience.

The prize will be sponsored
by faceless billionnaire 248
owner of plot 31744
the Communal Living Development
formerly known as Aintree.

What's the odds ?

It was a quiet evening
yesterday sitting by the fireside
listening to the music of the candles

a tealight symphony
of lavender and rose
harmony and counterpoint

as delicate as a Chopin nocturne
its fragrant melodies releasing
the serotonin and endorphins

carrying the mystical sound of
ylang ylang. A gentle breath of air

and a little sideways flicker
as if an invisible child had made
a birthday wish.

A few doors down an old woman
passed away. Lived alone
they said, in her nineties.

Husband died in the war, kept
herself to herself. Ellen they said,
or Helen maybe. Had a cat.

inset photo: War Memorial at Huyton-with-Roby

I'd like to bottle the Mersey air
and take it with me everywhere

I'd guard it like a royal jewel
to remind me of my Liverpool

I'd carry it on a foreign trip
to take as a medicinal sip

I'd bring it to the factory floor
and open it at my boss's door

I'd save some for my darkest hours
its scent to me like fresh-cut flowers

To prise my hand you'd best be brave
'cos I'm taking it with me to my grave

My city is amazin'
A jangle of people wherever yer gazin'...

The news is all around you
Not just on TV
Not just in soundbites fed to the community
By executives with immunity
From images of reality
Where truth becomes a rarity.
At the end of the day
The news is you and you and you and me.

It's time for re-appraisin'
My city is amazin'...

[... extract from 'Community']

ACKNOWLEDGEMENTS

The original full version of **A Million Suns** was highly commended in the 'Wirral Festival of Firsts' poetry competition, 2015, and was also published in the author's debut collection, **Bird's Eye View**.

Some of the poems/extracts have also appeared in the publications listed below.

Other Collections by the same author:

BIRD'S EYE VIEW
(anthology including several prize-winning and commended poems, recommended by New Writing North, Sept 2021)

TRIBUTE NIGHT AT THE SOCIAL
(3rd prize, Yeovil Writing Without Restrictions Competition, 2017)

WHISPER ON THE SHORE

TOUCHPOINTS

PAUSE AND REWIND
(series of photo-poems)

More poetry and verse and links to other creative arts can be found on:

www.burg34.com

Disclaimer: There is no unequivocal endorsement or any criticism implied with regards anywhere, anything or anyone mentioned in this book.

All character names used are entirely fictitious.